CALIFORNIA TRAVEL ACTIVITY BOOK AND JOURNAL

This book belongs to:
_____

First published in 2019 by Family A Go Go

Text and Illustration copyright © 2019 Family A Go Go

Written and Illustrated by: Lauren Kotwal

www.familyagogobooks.com

All Rights Reserved. No part of this publication may be reproduced, storied in a retrieval system, or transmitted by any form or by any means, electronic, recording or otherwise without the prior permission in writing from Family A Go Go.

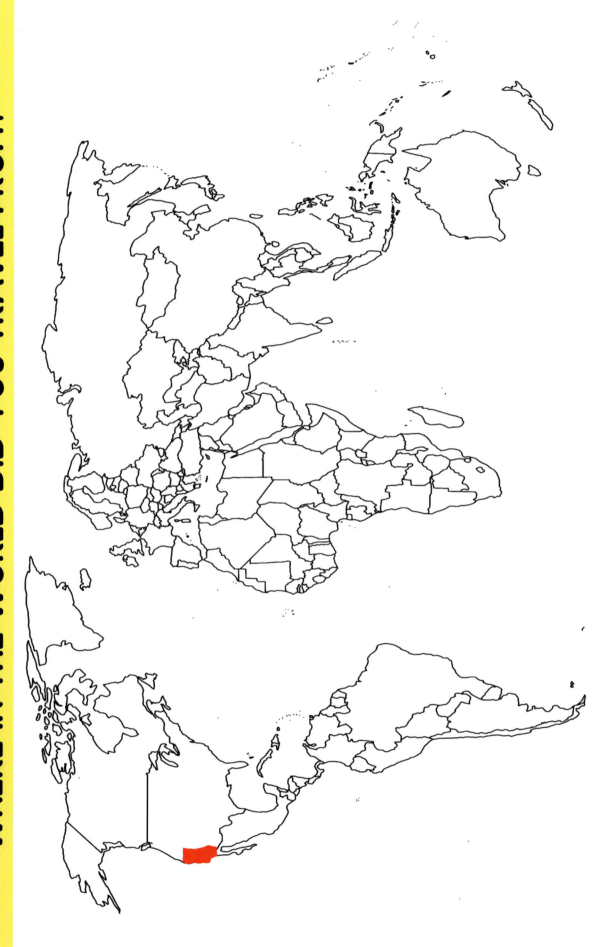

Bingo!

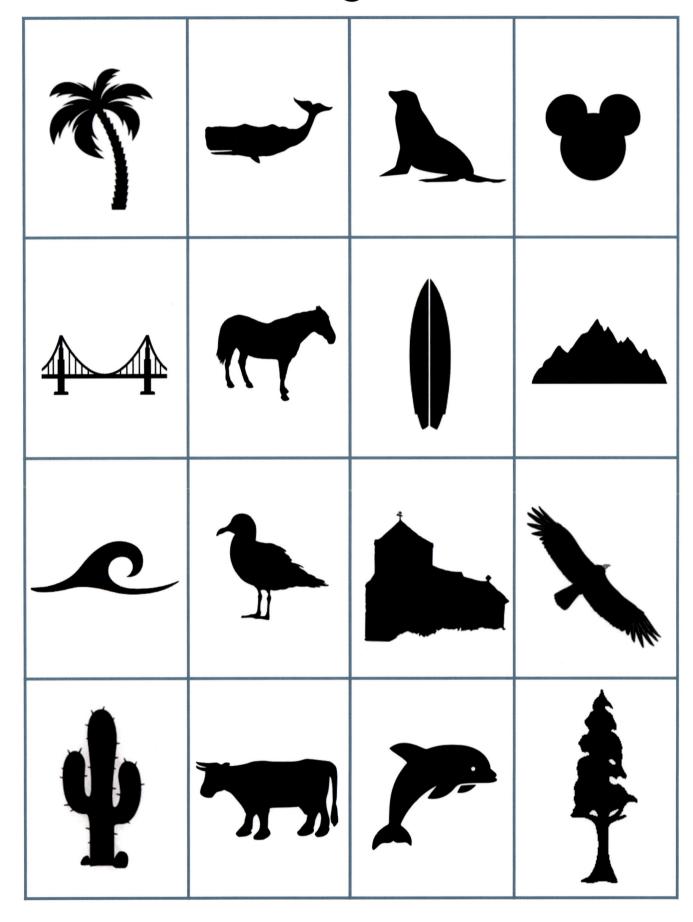

California History

More than 10,000 years ago, the first people arrived in what is now California. These people walked all the way from Asia using a strip of land called the Bering Strait. This area once connected the Asian continent to the North American continent, but it is now deep under water. These first settlers spread through North America. In California, there were over 500 Native tribes that lived all over the state.

In the 16th century, Spanish explorers began settling in California. They soon built over 20 missions and 4 presidios (fortresses) up and down the state. The first mission was the San Diego de Alcalá in San Diego in 1769. The Spanish settlement drastically changed the landscape and the lives of the Native People. The Spanish brought with them new diseases (that took the lives of many Native People) and took whatever land they wanted. This ended up greatly reducing the size of the Native tribes and their lands.

Mexico briefly gained control of the area in 1948, but after the Mexican-American War, California became a U.S. territory. In 1849, gold was found at Sutter's Mill in Northern California, and people flocked to the area to try and strike it rich. These people were nicknamed "forty-niners." Just a year later, in 1850, California officially became a state.

The name "California" comes from a 16th century Spanish novel that describes a mythical paradise called *California*

Color the CA State Flag

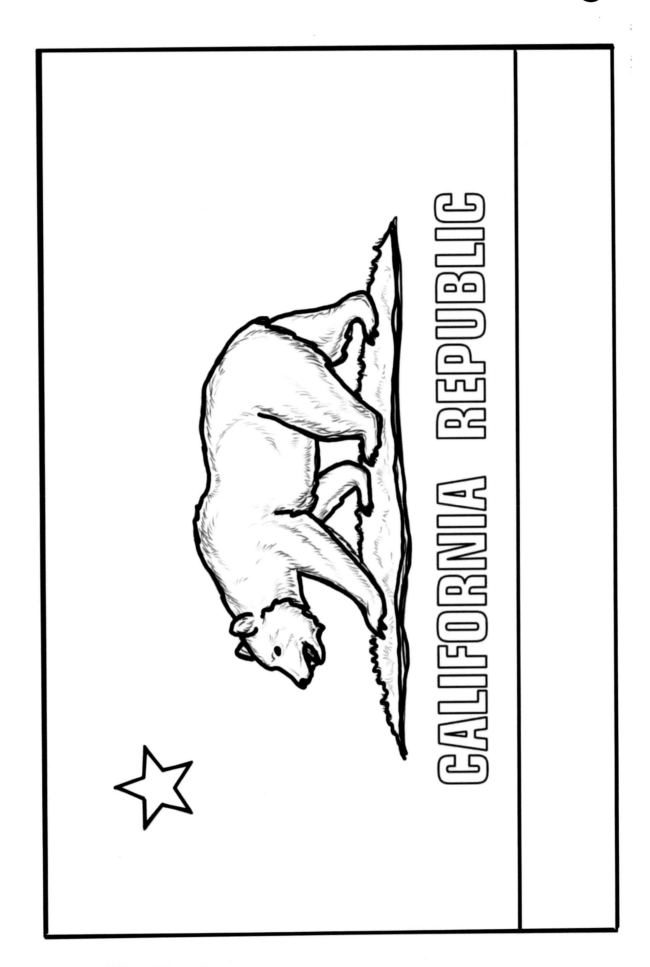

Draw the CA State Bird

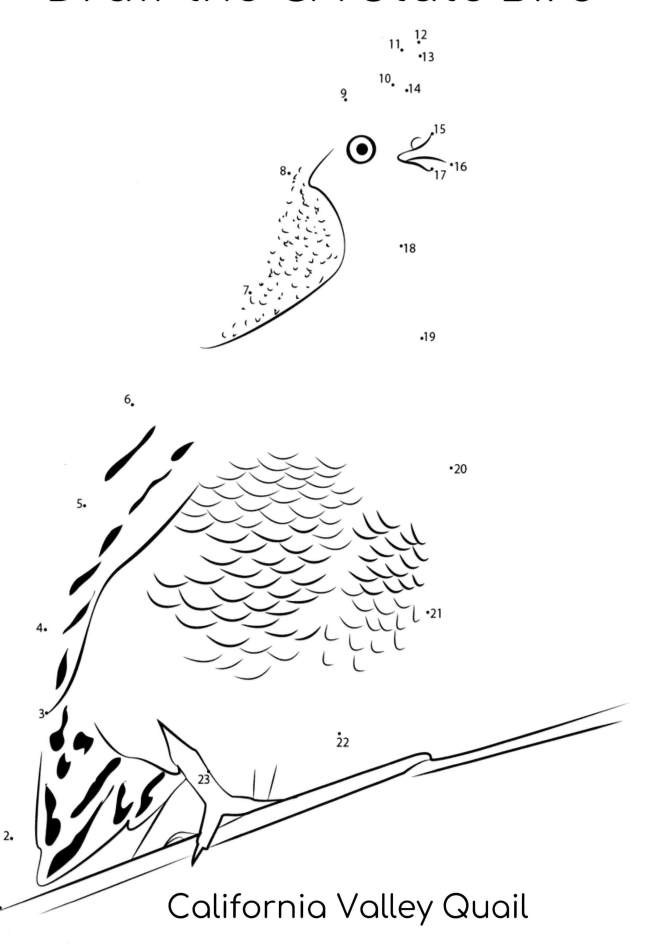

California Valley Quail

Beaches

If you like the beach, California is the place for you! You can find lots of different types of beaches depending on which part of the state you visit. From San Diego to Los Angeles, you will find many wide sandy beaches. As you move up the coast from Los Angeles, the beaches get narrower, but more dramatic, with towering cliffs and rocky beaches. Be prepared to see surfers, kiteboarders, paddle boarders, swimmers, and lots of people enjoying the beach.

Walking around the beaches around Santa Barbara may cause you to get tar stuck to your feet. Don't worry! It comes off easily with vegetable oil. Many people think the tar is from an oil spill that happened off the Santa Barbara coast in the 1970s, but it is actually just oil naturally seeping up from the ocean floor.

The coastline around the Bay Area north to the Oregon state border is wild and beautiful. The water is colder than down south, so outside of the major cities, you generally won't see too many other people on the beaches with you.

Up and down the coast, you will see lots of seabirds, seals, otters, sharks, dolphins, and whales (if you are extra lucky!)

Draw a picture of your family at the beach!

Tide Pools

Tide pools form when waves move down the beach at low tide, leaving some water and animals behind in rock pools. Look at tide charts to see when it will be low tide and go explore!

Rules for visiting tide pools

- **Be careful!** Watch where you step, don't run, and don't turn your back to the ocean!
- **Do not pry!** Many types of animals such as sea stars and sea urchins live attached to the rocks. Do not pry these off. If an animal is harder to pick up than a set of keys, then leave it where you found it.
- **Be Gentle!** Do not poke or prod the animals. Fingers can be used to touch gently. Wet your hands before touching any animals and use just two fingers.
- **No Collecting!** Leave only footprints, take only pictures and memories.

Draw things you could see in a CA tidepool

Mountains

The first thing you think of when you think of California may be the beach, but this state is home to many mountains and winter activities. If you are interested in skiing or snowboarding, check out Mammoth Lake, Squaw Valley, South Lake Tahoe, or Big Bear Lake.

Lake Tahoe is a large freshwater lake in the Sierra Nevada Mountains that lies on the California/Nevada border. The water is sparking blue and crystal clear. The lake was formed about 2 million years ago and was shaped during the ice age. There are activities to do here all year long, with ski and snowboarding in the winter and boating and hiking in the summer.

If you like hiking and want a challenge, look no further than Mt Whitney, which is the highest summit in the United States.

Help the skier find their way to the lodge!

Deserts

Deserts may seem like hot, sandy, empty places, but California deserts are often beautiful and full of life. Joshua Tree National Park has giant boulders and alien-like yucca plants. The Anza-Borrego state park (the largest State Park in CA) has beautiful springtime wildflower displays. The Palm Springs region has golf resorts, pools, the Living Desert, and windmills. And Death Valley's Badwater has the lowest elevation in North America, at 282 feet below sea level. The hottest air temperature ever recorded was here in 1913...134 degrees!

Did you know that some desert birds make their homes INSIDE of cacti? The Gila Woodpecker is well known for using its long beak to make holes in large saguaro cacti. They like to live in cacti because it provides a safe and cool place for them to raise their babies.

DRAW SOME BIRDS INSIDE OF THE SAGUARO CACTI

Wildlife

With a wide variety of habitats throughout California, there a lot of different types of animals here.

In the forests and fields, keep an eye out for black bears, mountain lions, bighorn sheep, wild pigs, deer, and elk. Search the skies for a sight of turkey vultures, California condors, and California quails (the state bird). By the ocean, see if you can spot California sea lions, sea otters, elephant seals, and blue whales. And in the desert regions, look for coyotes, jackrabbits, ground squirrels, lizards, and rattlesnakes.

While the California Grizzly is the State Animal of California, and is on the State Flag, it was hunted to extinction in 1924.

Match the animals with their footprints

Trees

About 6,500 different types of plants live in California. Some of the most impressive and unique types of plants here are the state's trees.

Joshua trees – Also called Yucca brevifolia, these are the tallest type of yucca and only grow in the Mojave Desert.

Coast Redwoods - These redwoods usually live 500-700 years, but it is possible for them live to more than 2,000 years and grow to over 360 feet in height!

Giant Sequoia - The world's biggest tree by volume is a giant sequoia in Sequoia National Park named General Sherman. It's 102 feet around (that's bigger than a basketball court!) and may be as many as 2,700 years old!

Palm trees – Palm trees were first planted by 18th century Franciscan missionaries and are now found all over southern California.

300 ft.

100 ft.

5-6 ft.

Coastal Redwood | 10 Story Building | Human

Fill in the tree

San Diego

San Diego is full of fun things to do for families. You could spend your whole vacation exploring different beaches all along the coast. You can take surf lessons, try some body boarding in the waves, and build sand castles on the beach. If you need a break from the beach, take a drive to Coronado Island, walk around downtown San Diego, explore the amazing San Diego Zoo, walk through the beautiful Balboa Park, watch the sea lions at the La Jolla Cove, or hike in the Torrey Pines State Reserve. In the northern part of the County, you will find quieter beach communities and places like the San Diego Zoo Safari Park and Legoland.

Like the rest of Southern California, San Diego is very large and spread out, so make sure to give yourself plenty of time when driving between activities.

Design some surfboards!

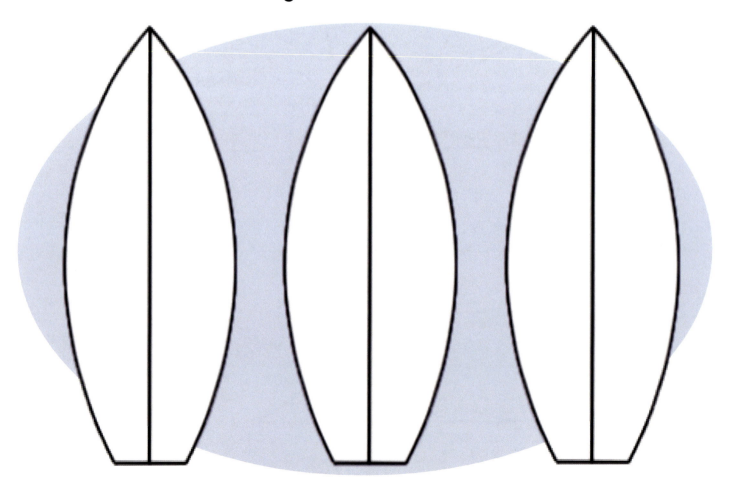

Los Angeles

Los Angeles was officially founded in 1542 by the Spanish. The discovery of oil in the 1890s brought huge growth to the area, and in the 1900s came the television and movie industry. Today it is the second biggest city in the US, after New York City.

There is so much to do in the Los Angeles region. You can see the stars on the Hollywood Walk of Fame, play games and go on rides on the Santa Monica Pier, visit the many amusements parks (like Disneyland), see the dinosaurs at the La Brea Tar pits, see the great views at the Griffith Observatory, hang out at the beach and people watch in Venice Beach, or explore the delicious food scene.

You will find even more to do and explore as you head south of Los Angeles. You can visit the Aquarium of the Pacific in Long Beach and explore the many beaches in places like Huntington Beach and Laguna Beach.

Draw your name below the Hollywood sign:

Skateboarding

Skateboarding was invented in California in the 1950s by people that wanted to surf when there were no waves. Skateboards were first made made from roller skates attached to a board and was called "sidewalk surfing."

In the late 1970s, the California drought forced homeowners to drain their pools. In Los Angeles, skaters searched for empty swimming pools to skate in. New tricks were invented daily, such as aerials, inverts, and the ollies.

Skating can now be enjoyed by children as young as two. You can find skateparks, camps, and lessons in cities throughout the state.

Design a skateboard!

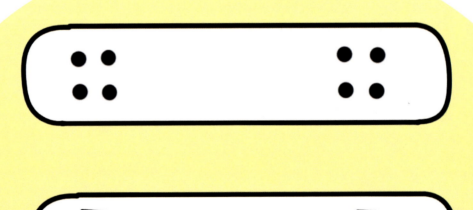

Central Coast

The Central Coast of California is a dream with beautiful beaches, tall cliffs, towering trees, and wild animals everywhere you look. The Central Coast is usually much quieter and calmer than Southern California. Here you will find the communities of Santa Barbara, Pismo Beach, Cambria, Carmel Valley, Monterey, and Santa Cruz.

In Santa Barbara, you can visit the beautiful Spanish-style County Courthouse, the historic Mission Santa Barbara, eat seafood and shop on Fisherman's wharf, see the beautiful zoo, and take a boat trip to see whales or go out to the Channel Islands. From Santa Barbara, you can drive up the scenic Route 1 up the coast. You can see the sand dunes in Pismo Beach, the elephant seals in Cambria, hike through the giant trees in Big Sur, and visit amazing Monterey Bay Aquarium.

Complete the patterns!

Bay Area and Northern CA

The Bay Area is considered part of Northern California, even though it is really in the center of the state. It includes all the cities that border the San Francisco bay. One of the most famous of these cities is San Francisco.

In San Francisco, be sure to visit the Golden Gate Bridge, Union Square, take a day trip to Alcatraz Island, have fun on Fisherman's Wharf, explore Chinatown, and check out museums like the Museum of Science and the Exploratorium. You can also take the subway (the BART) to the East Bay to see the University of California Berkeley, Telegraph Ave, and Lake Merritt in Oakland.

Further north you will find Muir Woods, Sausalito, the Napa Valley wine country, and Sonoma County. Drive out to the Point Reyes National Seashore to see the lighthouse, amazing views of the ocean, and elephant seals. At the very northern part of CA you will find the communities of Humboldt and Redding. Here you can find some of the largest giant Sequoias in the state. You can even drive your car through the trunk of one of them (the Tunnel Log in Sequoia National Park)!

Draw a cars and people on the Golden Gate Bridge

Yosemite National Park

Yosemite National Park is in the eastern potion of the state. It was designated as a national park in 1890 and spans 1,169 square miles. Here you will find breathtaking waterfalls, scenic views, meadows, and giant ancient sequoia trees, and many places to hike and explore. There are also giant granite rock formations that were shaped tens of thousands of years ago by moving glaciers.

Some of the biggest landmarks here are Half Dome and El Capitan. While you explore the park, keep your eyes peeled for bobcats, black bears, spotted owls, and kingsnakes.

If you visit Yosemite, make sure to stop by a Ranger Station and pick up either a Junior Ranger (ages 7-13) or Little Cub (ages 3-6) booklet. You can earn a patch if you complete the activities!

Yosemite Cave Pseudoscorpion

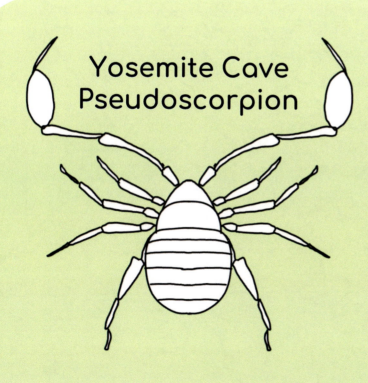

The Yosemite Cave pseudoscorpion is a species of spider that was discovered in 2010 living in the park's caves. This creature is about the length of a fingernail. It resembles a true scorpion, but it does not possess a stinger or a tail, and it is blind. This species is believed to only live in Yosemite and no where else in the world.

Finish drawing the animals

Decorate the butterflies

Draw a picture of what you did today

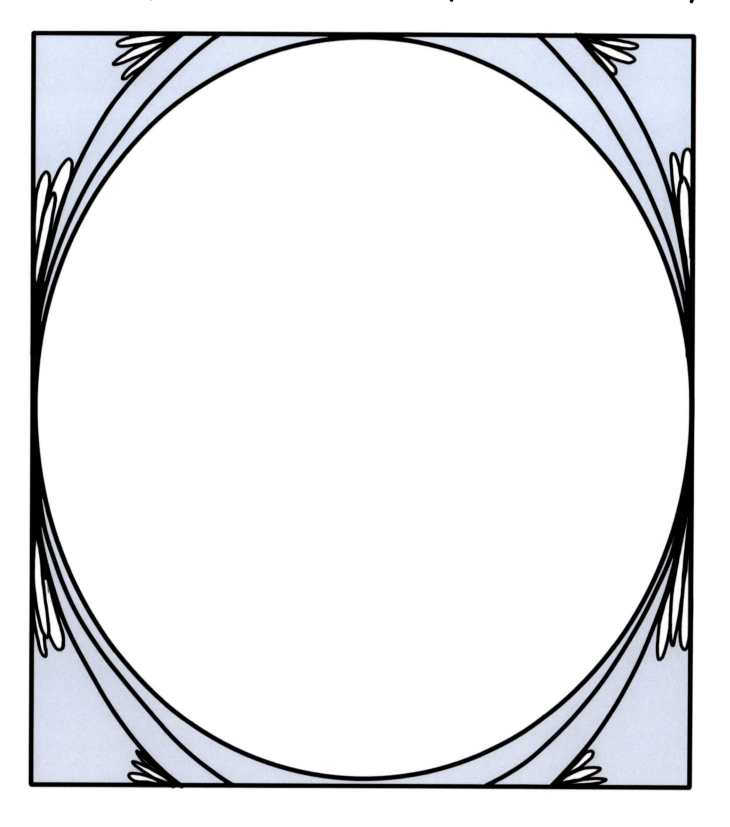

------------------------- . -----

Draw a picture of what you did today

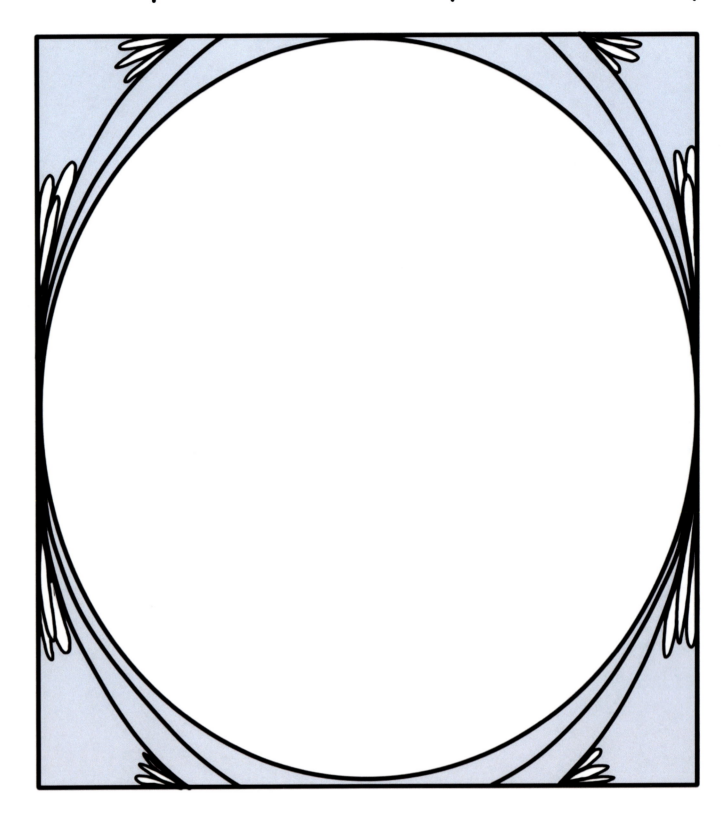

Draw a picture of what you did today

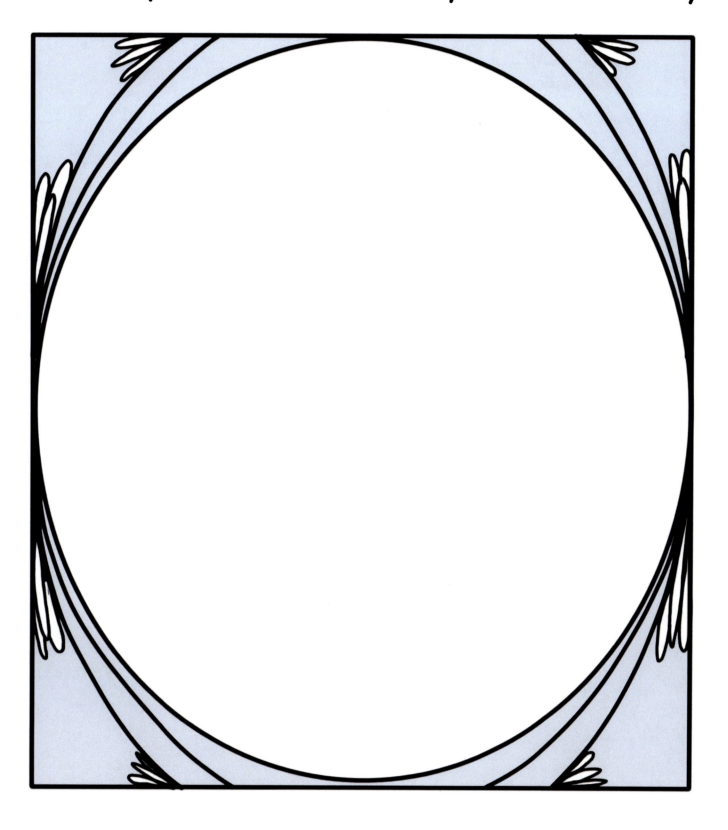

- - - - - - - - - - - - - - - - - - - .- - -

- -

Draw a picture of what you did today

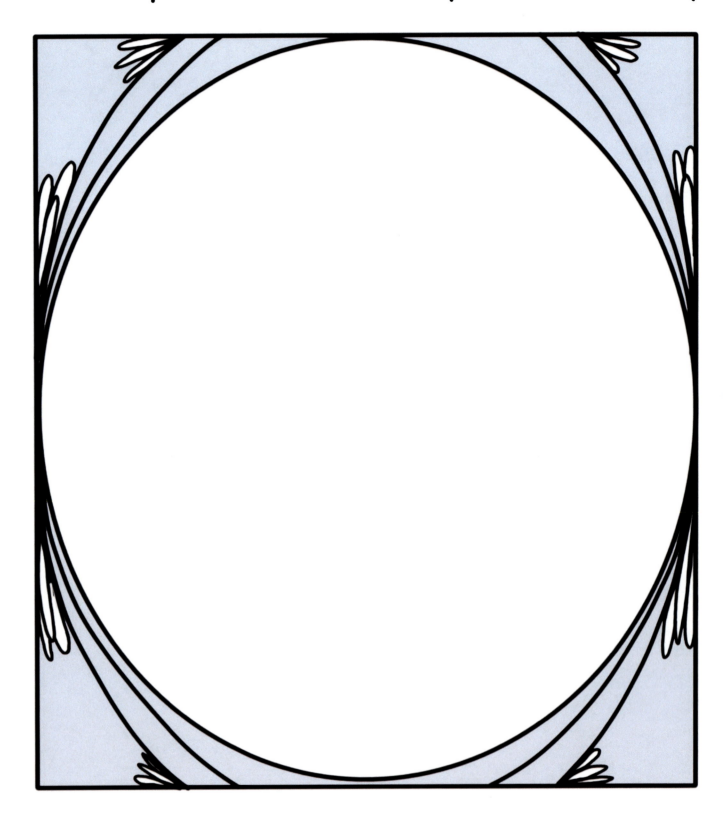

------------------------------ . --

Draw a picture of what you did today

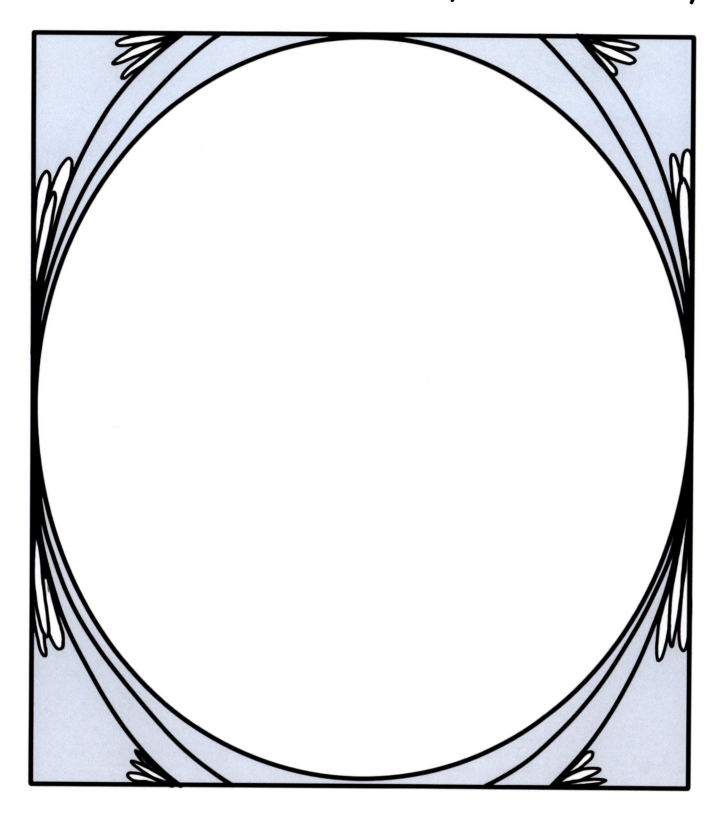

Draw a picture of what you did today

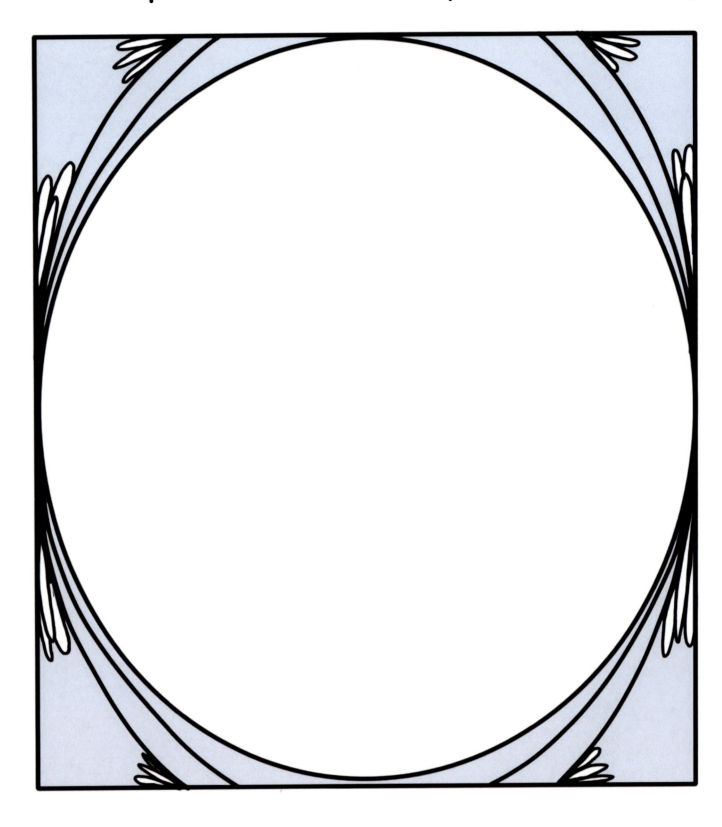

- - - - - - - - - - - - - - - - - - .- - -

- -

Draw the best thing you did!

Draw the best thing you did!

Draw the best place you stayed!

Doodle Page!

Doodle Page!

Doodle Page!

Made in the USA
Columbia, SC
26 January 2022